BREAK YOUR MOLD
THE WORKBOOK

THIS BOOK IS AVAILABLE AT SPECIAL QUANTITY DISCOUNTS FOR BULK PURCHASE FOR SALES PROMOTIONS, PREMIUMS, FUND-RAISING, AND EDUCATIONAL NEEDS. FOR DETAILS EMAIL ROLAND@ROLANDBYRD.COM.

ISBN 13: 978-1-940324-05-0

ISBN 10: 194032405X

BREAK YOUR MOLD
THE WORKBOOK
THE ART OF OVERCOMING PATTERNS AND BEHAVIORS THAT HOLD YOU BACK.

By

Roland Byrd

Congratulations!

You're embarking on an amazing adventure!

Break Your Mold: The Workbook contains all the life-changing exercises from the Transformational book, Break Your Mold: The Art of Overcoming Patterns and Behaviors That Hold You Back.

If you're reading the eBook version of Break Your Mold, this workbook allows you to do the exercises without the fuss of having to print out every worksheet.

If you're reading the print version of Break Your Mold, this workbook allows you the freedom of doing the exercises more than once. It also gives you the choice whether to write in your book or not.

I've provided ample space for you to jot down notes. That way you can keep track of your insights and other thoughts as you do the exercises.

Enjoy the book! Enjoy the process! And most of all, *Enjoy Life!*

You Are The Master of Your Destiny!

Roland

P.S. If you order more than one workbook you can do the exercises along with your significant other, family, or even friends!

The Kindle version of Break Your Mold: The Art of Overcoming Patterns and Behaviors That Hold You Back is available here: http://bit.ly/BreakYourMoldKindle

The print version is available here: http://bit.ly/BreakYourMold

MY PERFECT LIFE QUESTIONS

For the next two minutes, think about your perfect life. Imagine your life if nothing held you back, if all your dreams came true.

Got it?

Good. Now answer the following questions:

What does it look like?

_____
_____
_____
_____
_____
_____
_____

What colors are there?

_____
_____
_____
_____
_____
_____

What does it feel like?

_____
_____
_____
_____

What is its texture?

_____
_____
_____
_____
_____
_____

What does it smell like?

_____
_____
_____
_____
_____
_____
_____

What plants, perfumes, foods, or nature can you smell?

_____
_____
_____
_____
_____
_____

What does it sound like?

_____
_____
_____
_____

Is it calm and peaceful or busy and bustling?

_____

_____

_____

_____

_____

_____

_____

Or, is it busy yet peaceful?

_____

_____

_____

_____

_____

_____

_____

Who shares your perfect life with you?

_____

_____

_____

_____

_____

_____

Notes:

MY PERFECT LIFE

Using your answers from the My Perfect Life Questions worksheet, go ahead and write a few paragraphs about your perfect life on the next page. Take a deep breath, relax, and describe your perfect life in as much detail as you can.

_____
_____
_____
_____
_____
_____
_____
_____
_____
_____
_____
_____
_____
_____
_____
_____
_____
_____
_____
_____
_____
_____
_____
_____
_____
_____
_____

_____

_____

_____

_____

_____

_____

_____

_____

_____

_____

_____

_____

_____

_____

_____

_____

_____

_____

_____

_____

_____

_____

_____

_____

Now sign your name.

_____

MY OBSTACLES

First, take a few minutes right now, and write down all the obstacles in your life. Obstacles are the things that keep you from getting what you want out of life.

_____

_____

_____

_____

_____

_____

_____

_____

_____

_____

_____

_____

_____

_____

_____

_____

_____

_____

_____

_____

_____

_____

_____

_____

_____

_____

_____

_____

_____

_____

_____

_____

_____

_____

_____

_____

_____

_____

_____

_____

_____

_____

_____

_____

_____

_____

_____

_____

_____

_____

_____

_____

_____

Notes:

MY ACTION ITEMS

Write down at least one action item for each obstacle that is in your control—from the My Obstacles Worksheet. These should be small, manageable things that you can take action on immediately.

_____
_____
_____
_____
_____
_____
_____
_____
_____
_____
_____
_____
_____
_____
_____
_____
_____
_____
_____
_____
_____
_____
_____
_____
_____
_____
_____

Please sign your name

_____

Thank you!

Now that you've listed your action items, pick the easiest one on the list and *do it now*.

Yes. You read that right. **Do it now.**

This creates feelings of success and tells your subconscious mind *you're serious about changing your life*.

WHAT HURTS IN MY LIFE?

Write down all the things that hurt or bother you in your life. Every answer is correct. Just write them below.

_____

_____

_____

_____

_____

_____

_____

_____

_____

_____

_____

_____

_____

_____

_____

_____

_____

_____

_____

Notes:

MY REALIZATIONS

Ask yourself the question about each pain point you listed before; "Why am I feeling (*pain, aggravation, anger, sadness, depression, etc.*) about that?" Now ask that question about each answer you get until you run out of answers! The last answer you receive is almost always the root cause of that pain point. (It might help to print one of these sheets for each pain point.)

_____
_____
_____
_____
_____
_____
_____
_____
_____
_____
_____
_____
_____
_____
_____
_____
_____
_____
_____
_____
_____
_____
_____

Notes:

WHAT I WANT

Review each root pain point and ask yourself, "What do I want?" Make sure your answers are only about what you want. That keeps your focus on the outcome you desire, which is key to creating lasting change!

Please write your answers here:

_____
_____
_____
_____
_____
_____
_____
_____
_____
_____
_____
_____
_____
_____
_____
_____
_____
_____
_____
_____
_____
_____
_____
_____
_____
_____
_____
_____
_____
_____

_____
_____
_____
_____
_____
_____
_____
_____
_____
_____
_____
_____
_____
_____
_____
_____
_____
_____
_____
_____
_____
_____
_____
_____
_____
_____
_____
_____

Now please sign your name:

_____

GOOD THINGS ABOUT FEAR

Fear can be positive. Take a moment and let your creative mind reveal some good things about fear.

Got some?

Great! Write those here:

_____

_____

_____

_____

_____

_____

_____

_____

_____

_____

_____

_____

_____

_____

_____

_____

_____

_____

_____

_____

_____

_____

_____

_____

_____

_____

_____

_____

Notes:

EXPANDING MY COMFORT ZONE

What's something you can do to expand your comfort zone?

    Got it?

    Great! Write it here:

_____

_____

_____

_____

_____

_____

_____

_____

_____

_____

_____

_____

_____

_____

_____

_____

_____

_____

_____

_____

_____

    Now sign your name:

_____

Notes:

MY LINES IN THE SAND

What are some of the lines you've drawn in the sand?

Go ahead and write them here:

_____

_____

_____

_____

_____

_____

_____

_____

_____

_____

_____

_____

_____

_____

_____

_____

_____

_____

_____

_____

_____

_____

_____

_____

_____

_____

_____

_____

_____

_____

_____

_____

_____

_____

_____

_____

_____

_____

_____

_____

_____

_____

_____

_____

_____

Notes:

MY OLD BEHAVIORS

Take a moment and think of one or two behaviors *you must stop doing*. If there are more, that's okay. You can list them too.

Now write them here:

_____

_____

_____

_____

_____

_____

_____

_____

_____

_____

_____

_____

_____

_____

_____

_____

_____

_____

_____

_____

_____

Notes:

Notes:

MY NEW BEHAVIORS

Now that you've written the behaviors you want to change (on the My Old Behaviors Worksheet), take a moment and think of the opposite of each behavior. For example; if you want to *stop overeating*, you might think, "I want to eat healthy portions of food." Or, "I want to stop eating when I feel comfortably full."

You get the idea.

Have you got them?

Great!

Write your new, healthier behaviors here:

_____

_____

_____

_____

_____

_____

_____

_____

_____

_____

_____

_____

_____

_____

_____

_____

_____

_____

_____

_____

_____

_____

_____

_____

_____

_____

_____

_____

_____

_____

_____

_____

_____

_____

_____

_____

_____

_____

_____

_____

_____

_____

_____

_____

_____

_____

_____

Now sign your name:

_____

I'M IN THE PROCESS OF MASTERING

Think about something (or things) you'd like to improve. It can be anything.

Have you got it?

Great!

Write it or them here:

_____
_____
_____
_____
_____
_____
_____
_____
_____
_____
_____
_____
_____
_____
_____
_____
_____
_____
_____
_____
_____
_____
_____
_____
_____
_____

Since you're in the process of mastering the thing(s) you listed on the previous page, it's critical you notice the things that are going right. Take notes on this page about everything that's going well, everything that works, and all the little successes you have when you're working on mastering your skill.

MY MASTERY NOTES

_____
_____
_____
_____
_____
_____
_____
_____
_____
_____
_____
_____
_____
_____
_____
_____
_____
_____
_____
_____
_____
_____
_____
_____
_____
_____
_____
_____
_____
_____
_____
_____

LEARNING FROM THE PAST

It's time to use the following five questions to help you create a better future!

"What have I done to get here?"

"What lessons are in this for me?"

"How can I use the knowledge I've gained from this to make life better?"

"How can I use the knowledge I've gained from this to help others?"

"If I'm in a similar situation in the future, what must I do differently?"

First think of something you regret or could have handled differently. Then answer all the questions to the best of your ability. Remember, there's no right or wrong here.

Something I Regret or Could Have Handled Differently

_____

_____

_____

_____

_____

_____

_____

_____

_____

_____

_____

_____

_____

_____

_____

Notes:

1. What have I done to get here?

This allows you to become aware of choices you made and things you did that helped create the situation you described. If it helps you can rephrase the question to, "What did I do to get there?"

Write your choices and actions here:

My Choices and Actions

_____
_____
_____
_____
_____
_____
_____
_____
_____
_____
_____
_____
_____
_____
_____
_____
_____
_____
_____
_____
_____
_____
_____
_____
_____
_____
_____

2. What lessons are in this for me?

Please write the lessons you've learned—or can learn—from the situation here:

My Lessons

_____

_____

_____

_____

_____

_____

_____

_____

_____

_____

_____

_____

_____

_____

_____

_____

_____

_____

_____

_____

_____

_____

_____

_____

_____

_____

_____

3. How can I use the knowledge I've gained from this to make my life better?

Write your answers—about how you can use the knowledge you've gained from the situation to make your life better—here:

Knowledge I've Gained

_____

_____

_____

_____

_____

_____

_____

_____

_____

_____

_____

_____

_____

_____

_____

_____

_____

_____

_____

_____

_____

_____

_____

_____

_____

_____

_____

_____

_____

_____

_____

_____

4. How can I use the knowledge I've gained from this to help others?

Please write your answers here:

How I'll Use My Knowledge to Help Others

_____

_____

_____

_____

_____

_____

_____

_____

_____

_____

_____

_____

_____

_____

_____

_____

_____

_____

_____

_____

_____

_____

_____

_____

_____

_____

_____

5. If I'm in a similar situation in the future, what must I do differently?

On this question it's vital you write what you'll do differently instead of what you won't do. Instead of saying, "I won't yell at my wife or husband." Say, "I'll remain calm and keep my voice under control." That tells your subconscious mind that remaining calm and keeping your voice under control are what's important.

Go ahead and write your answer here:

What I'll do Differently in the Future

_____
_____
_____
_____
_____
_____
_____
_____
_____
_____
_____
_____
_____
_____
_____
_____
_____
_____
_____
_____
_____
_____
_____
_____
_____

_____

_____

_____

_____

_____

_____

_____

_____

_____

_____

_____

_____

_____

_____

_____

_____

_____

_____

Notes:

MY SELF-TALK

Have you ever listened to how you talk to yourself?

Are you kind? Or are you mean?

Go ahead and pay attention to what you say to yourself. Start consciously listening to your self-talk.

You might be surprised at what you discover.

For the next Twenty-Four hours, document the things you say to yourself on a regular basis here:

_____
_____
_____
_____
_____
_____
_____
_____
_____
_____
_____
_____
_____
_____
_____
_____
_____
_____
_____
_____
_____
_____
_____
_____

_____

_____

_____

_____

_____

_____

_____

_____

_____

_____

_____

_____

_____

_____

_____

_____

_____

Great! Now please answer the following questions about your self-talk.

"Are there patterns in what I say to myself?"

Please list them:

_____

_____

_____

_____

_____

_____

_____

"How do I feel when I say these things to myself?"

_____

_____

_____

_____

_____

_____

"If I heard someone talking to another the way I talk to myself, what would I think?"

_____

_____

_____

"Would I think they were too harsh?"

_____

_____

_____

"Would I think they were mean?"

_____

_____

_____

"Would I think they were angry at the other person?"

_____

_____

_____

"Would I think they should give the other person some slack?"

_____

_____

_____

And here's the most important question. "Do I want to treat myself that way?"

_____

_____

_____

Notes:

MY EMPOWERING SELF-TALK STATEMENTS

Following the direction in the book, write your new, empowering self-talk statements here:

_____

_____

_____

_____

_____

_____

_____

_____

_____

_____

_____

_____

_____

_____

_____

_____

_____

_____

_____

_____

_____

_____

_____

_____

_____

_____

_____

_____

_____

_____

Notes:

I COULD HAVE HANDLED THIS DIFFERENTLY

First, you'll think of something that happened in the past few days that you could have resolved differently. Then we'll apply the following questions to it.

"Was my reaction warranted?"

"What emotions influenced my reaction?"

"What is it in my history that fueled this reaction?"

"Was this situation really what it seemed?"

"How could I have respond effectively to this situation?"

Do you have the situation you want to use in mind?

Great! Please write it here:

_____
_____
_____
_____
_____
_____
_____
_____
_____
_____
_____
_____
_____
_____
_____

_____

_____

_____

_____

_____

_____

_____

_____

_____

_____

_____

_____

_____

_____

_____

_____

_____

_____

_____

_____

_____

Notes:

Great! Now, thinking of the situation you wrote above, please answer the following questions.

"Was my reaction warranted?"

Meaning did you overreact or underreact—yes underacting is possible—to the situation.

Write your answer and give a brief explanation here:

_____

_____

_____

_____

_____

_____

_____

_____

_____

_____

"What emotions influenced my reaction?"

Did you feel fear, anger, cornered, defensive, hurt, sad, helpless, etc.

Write your answer and a brief explanation here:

_____

_____

_____

_____

_____

_____

_____

_____

_____

"What is it in my history that fueled this reaction?"

Meaning; what event(s) or experience(s) from your past taught you that you should feel the way you did about the situation. This could be a single event or a pattern of behavior you experienced.

Write your answer and a brief explanation here:

_____

_____

_____

_____

_____

_____

_____

_____

_____

"Is this situation really what it seems?"

Remember how your brain looks for similarities and then offers reactions it thinks fit the situation? *Just because similarities exist doesn't mean the situation is the same.* Nor does it mean your learned reaction is appropriate.

This questions helps you recognize that the situation you reacted to might be very different from what you thought. And it helps your understanding that *consciously responding to situations gives you power to recognize differences and act accordingly.*

Write your answer and a brief explanation here:

_____

_____

_____

_____

_____

_____

_____

_____

_____

_____

_____

_____

"How could I have responded effectively to this situation?"

This powerful question gives you the chance to discover a different, effective response to the situation. When you do this it offers your subconscious mind an alternative for handling similar situations in the future. It gives you the power to choose your response. Think of it as retraining your subconscious mind.

Write your answer and a brief explanation here:

_____

_____

_____

_____

_____

_____

_____

_____

_____

_____

Since we're looking at or dealing with a past event, let's ask one more question.

"How will I respond to similar events in the future?"

This helps pre-script your subconscious mind with the idea that you'll respond instead of react to similar situations in the future. It also plants seeds for how you'll respond.

Write your answer here along with a brief explanation:

_____

_____

_____

_____

_____

_____

_____

_____

_____

_____

_____

Notes:

MY EMOTIONAL BASELINE

Date_____

What's your emotional baseline? How do you feel most of the time? Are you happy, sad, aggravated, angry, lonely, grateful, loving..?

Go ahead; write it, and brief explanation why, here:

_____

_____

_____

_____

_____

_____

_____

_____

_____

_____

_____

_____

_____

_____

_____

_____

_____

_____

_____

_____

_____

_____

_____

_____

_____

_____

_____

_____

_____

Notes:

MY THOUGHTS ABOUT MONEY

Take a moment and write down the first things that come to mind when I say, "Money". Reserve judgment, just write them down.

Deal?

Great! Go ahead and write them here:

_____
_____
_____
_____
_____
_____
_____
_____
_____
_____
_____
_____
_____
_____
_____
_____
_____
_____
_____
_____
_____
_____
_____
_____
_____
_____
_____
_____
_____
_____
_____
_____

My Emotions about Money

Now take a moment and write down all emotions your thoughts about "Money" evoked. Again, reserve judgment; just write them down as best you can.

_____

_____

_____

_____

_____

_____

_____

_____

_____

_____

_____

_____

_____

_____

_____

_____

_____

_____

_____

_____

_____

_____

_____

_____

_____

_____

_____

_____

_____

My Thoughts about Rich People

Take a moment and write down the first things that come to mind when I say, "Rich People". Remember; write them down without judgment.

_____

_____

_____

_____

_____

_____

_____

_____

_____

_____

_____

_____

_____

_____

_____

_____

_____

_____

_____

_____

_____

_____

_____

_____

_____

_____

_____

_____

_____

_____

_____

_____

_____

_____

_____

My Emotions about Rich People

Just like we did before, let's take a moment and write down emotions your thoughts about "Rich People" evoked. Again, write them down as best you can and withhold judgment.

_____

_____

_____

_____

_____

_____

_____

_____

_____

_____

_____

_____

_____

_____

_____

_____

_____

_____

_____

_____

_____

_____

_____

_____

_____

_____

_____

_____

_____

_____

_____

_____

_____

If you were honest, and if you really want to change there's every reason you should be, the thoughts and emotions you wrote reveal your subconscious beliefs about money.

Do your subconscious beliefs about money match your conscious desire for money?

Most people say, "No", but in some cases it's, "Yes".

Which is it for you?

Notes:

Notes:

THE PREVAILING MESSAGES I GIVE MY SUBCONSCIOUS MIND

What are you feeding your mind? What are the prevailing messages you give your subconscious?

Take a moment. Think of the music you like, the shows you watch, the things you read, and the topics of conversation you have.

Now write them down here:

_____
_____
_____
_____
_____
_____
_____
_____
_____
_____
_____
_____
_____
_____
_____
_____
_____
_____
_____
_____
_____
_____
_____
_____
_____

MY EMOTIONAL FLEXIBILITY

How emotionally flexible are you?

Take a moment and rate your emotional flexibility with the following true or false questions:

1. When something unplanned happens I feel anxious:

   True   False

2. Spontaneous events bother or annoy me:

   True   False

3. I like doing the same things most of the time:

   True   False

4. I like things my way:

   True   False

5. I'm rarely open to other's opinions:

   True   False

6. I usually follow a daily routine:

   True   False

7. I dislike new situations & unexpected events:

   True   False

What did your answers reveal? Are you adaptable or spontaneous? Or do you prefer to control situations and know exactly what's going to happen?

If you answered, "True" to 2 or more of the questions, then you're most likely a person who could work on their emotional flexibility.

Notes:

MY ACTION

Ask yourself, "What can I do, *Right Now*, to take action on changing my life?"

It doesn't need to be something grand. It might be and it's ok if it is. Something small works too. The key is to *do something*, to *take action*, tell your mind you're serious about changing your life!

Please write your action here:

_____

_____

_____

_____

_____

_____

_____

_____

_____

_____

_____

_____

_____

_____

_____

_____

_____

_____

_____

_____

_____

Now please sign your name: (*And then Go Do It!*)

_____

Notes:

MY PERFECT LIFE KEY POINTS

Using what you wrote for "My Perfect Life" in chapter 1, write down the key accomplishments or aspects of your perfect life—I'll provide space.

For example; if you wrote, "In my perfect life I have many good friends who love and support me and I have a job I love. I own a beautiful home and a nice car." Then in the space provided you might write:

I have many good friends who love and support me.

I have a job I love.

I own a beautiful home.

I own a nice car.

Got it?

Great!

Now please take a moment and write the key points from your perfect life here:

_____

_____

_____

_____

_____

_____

_____

_____

_____

_____

_____

_____

_____

_____

MY PERFECT LIFE

Using the space on the next few pages, write one paragraph—or one sentence—about each key point from your "My Perfect Life" exercise. I'll include the opening and closing statements for you.

My Perfect Life

I am in the process of attracting all that I need to do, know, or have to create my Perfect Life.

_____
_____
_____
_____
_____
_____
_____
_____
_____
_____
_____
_____
_____
_____
_____
_____
_____
_____
_____
_____
_____
_____
_____
_____
_____
_____
_____
_____

God, the universe, and the power of my expectations are unfolding and orchestrating all that needs to happen to create My Perfect Life!

I deserve My Perfect Life because I'm me!

I deserve My Perfect Life because I'm a perfect creation of God!

I deserve My Perfect Life because I use my abundance to help others!

I deserve My Perfect Life because it allows me to achieve my full potential!

I deserve My Perfect Life because _____

I deserve My Perfect Life because _____

I deserve My Perfect Life because _____

Sign Here: _____

Notes:

MY THINGS TO CELEBRATE

Five things I'm celebrating today:

1. _____
   _____
   _____
   _____

2. _____
   _____
   _____
   _____

3. _____
   _____
   _____
   _____

4. _____
   _____
   _____
   _____

5. _____
   _____
   _____
   _____

Hint... You should do this every day! So I've added week's worth of pages. That will get you started.

If you want, I've also greated a *My Celbrations & Success Journal with 90 day's worth of pages* that you can order here: http://bit.ly/BreakYourMoldSuccessJournal

Five things I'm celebrating today:

1. _____

   _____

   _____

   _____

2. _____

   _____

   _____

   _____

3. _____

   _____

   _____

   _____

4. _____

   _____

   _____

   _____

5. _____

   _____

   _____

   _____

Notes:

Five things I'm celebrating today:

1. _____
_____
_____
_____

2. _____
_____
_____
_____

3. _____
_____
_____
_____

4. _____
_____
_____
_____

5. _____
_____
_____
_____

Notes:

Five things I'm celebrating today:

1. _____
   _____
   _____
   _____

2. _____
   _____
   _____
   _____

3. _____
   _____
   _____
   _____

4. _____
   _____
   _____
   _____

5. _____
   _____
   _____
   _____

Notes:

Five things I'm celebrating today:

1. _____
_____
_____
_____

2. _____
_____
_____
_____

3. _____
_____
_____
_____

4. _____
_____
_____
_____

5. _____
_____
_____
_____

Notes:

Five things I'm celebrating today:

1. _____
   _____
   _____
   _____
   _____

2. _____
   _____
   _____
   _____
   _____

3. _____
   _____
   _____
   _____
   _____

4. _____
   _____
   _____
   _____

5. _____
   _____
   _____
   _____

Notes:

Five things I'm celebrating today:

1. _____
   _____
   _____
   _____

2. _____
   _____
   _____
   _____

3. _____
   _____
   _____
   _____

4. _____
   _____
   _____
   _____

5. _____
   _____
   _____
   _____

Notes:

Notes:

MY DAILY SUCCESS LOG

Five things I Succeeded at Today:

1. _____
_____
_____
_____

2. _____
_____
_____
_____

3. _____
_____
_____
_____

4. _____
_____
_____
_____

5. _____
_____
_____
_____

Hint... You should do this every day! So I've added six more pages. That way you can print a week's worth at a time.

If you want, I've also greated a *My Celbrations & Success Journal with 90 day's worth of pages* that you can order here: http://bit.ly/BreakYourMoldSuccessJournal

Five things I Succeeded at Today:

1. _____
   _____
   _____
   _____

2. _____
   _____
   _____
   _____

3. _____
   _____
   _____
   _____

4. _____
   _____
   _____
   _____

5. _____
   _____
   _____
   _____

Notes:

Five things I Succeeded at Today:

1. _____

_____

_____

_____

2. _____

_____

_____

_____

3. _____

_____

_____

_____

4. _____

_____

_____

_____

5. _____

_____

_____

_____

Notes:

Five things I Succeeded at Today:

1. _____
   _____
   _____
   _____

2. _____
   _____
   _____
   _____

3. _____
   _____
   _____
   _____

4. _____
   _____
   _____
   _____

5. _____
   _____
   _____
   _____

Notes:

Five things I Succeeded at Today:

1. _____
   _____
   _____
   _____

2. _____
   _____
   _____
   _____

3. _____
   _____
   _____
   _____

4. _____
   _____
   _____
   _____

5. _____
   _____
   _____
   _____

Notes:

Five things I Succeeded at Today:

1. _____
   _____
   _____
   _____

2. _____
   _____
   _____
   _____

3. _____
   _____
   _____
   _____

4. _____
   _____
   _____
   _____

5. _____
   _____
   _____
   _____

Notes:

Five things I Succeeded at Today:

1. _____
   _____
   _____
   _____

2. _____
   _____
   _____
   _____

3. _____
   _____
   _____
   _____

4. _____
   _____
   _____
   _____

5. _____
   _____
   _____
   _____

Notes:

Notes:

Notes:

Notes:

Notes:

Notes:

www.ingramcontent.com/pod-product-compliance
Lightning Source LLC
Chambersburg PA
CBHW081227040426
42445CB00016B/1908